A B C D E
F G H I J K
L M N O P
Q R S T U
V W X Y Z

For Friendship and Understanding

French~English Alphabet

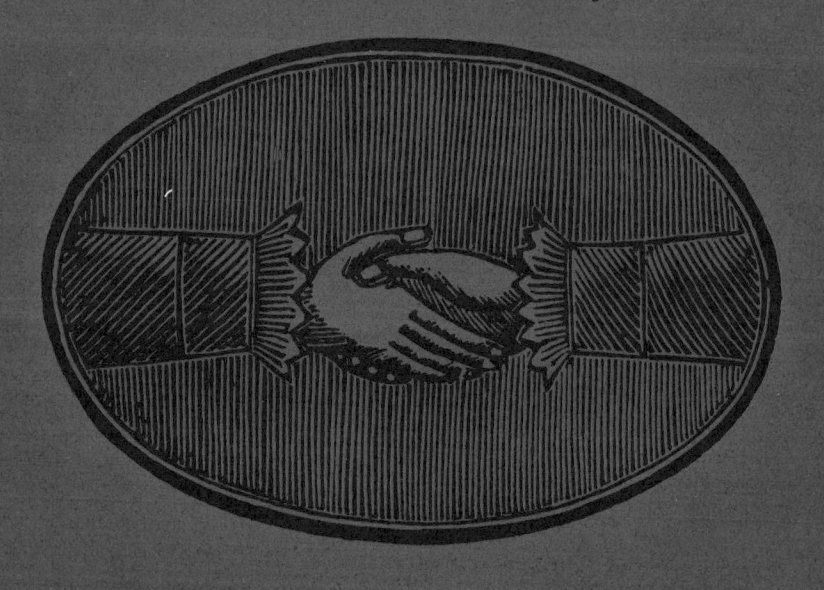

bouquet de fleurs

flower bouquet

A Friendly

A B C

French~English Alphabet

Illustrations by LORENZ FROELICH

Text by BENTE HAMANN

Frederick Warne and Company, Inc.

New York and London

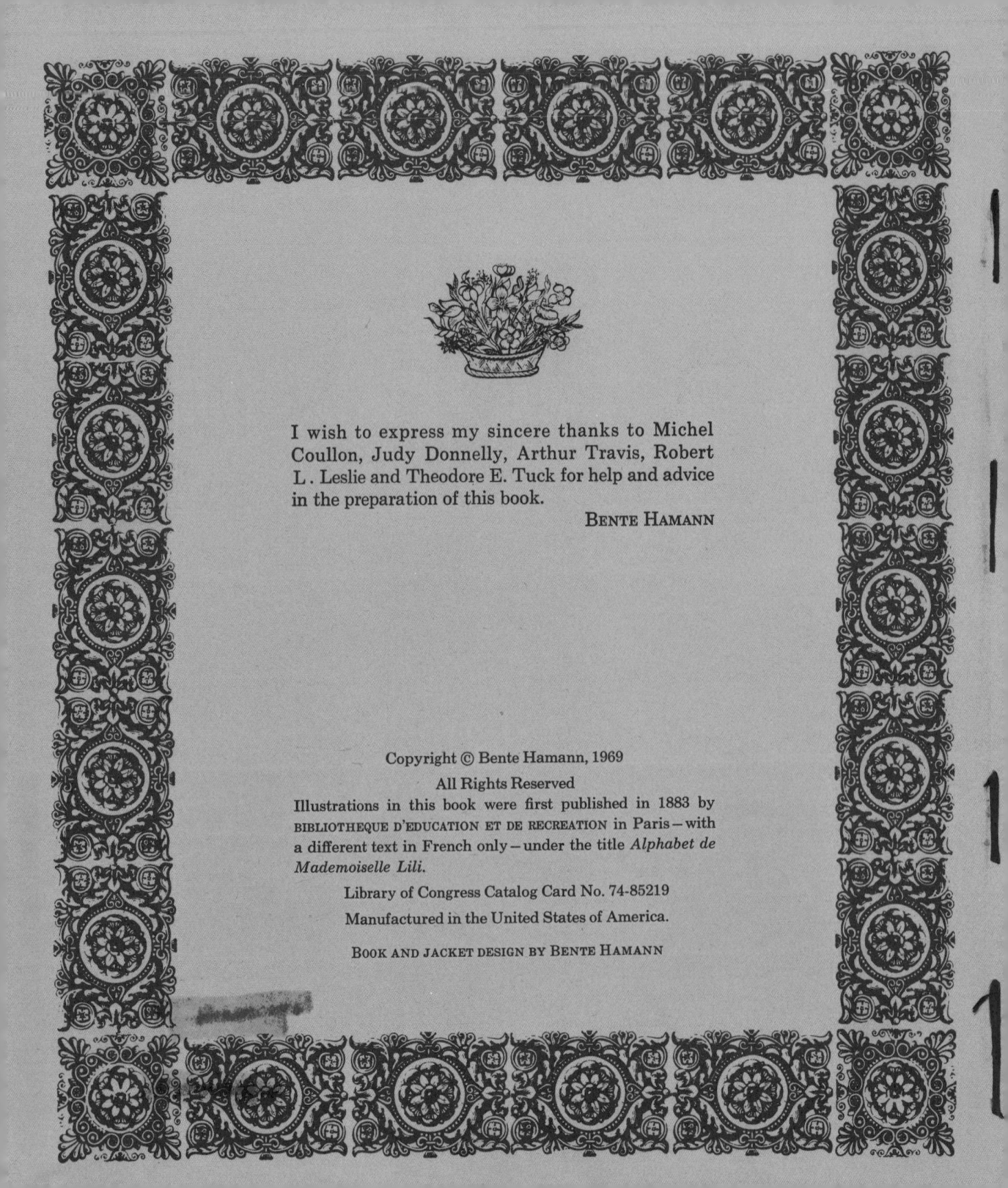

I wish to express my sincere thanks to Michel Coullon, Judy Donnelly, Arthur Travis, Robert L. Leslie and Theodore E. Tuck for help and advice in the preparation of this book.

BENTE HAMANN

Copyright © Bente Hamann, 1969

All Rights Reserved

Illustrations in this book were first published in 1883 by BIBLIOTHEQUE D'EDUCATION ET DE RECREATION in Paris — with a different text in French only — under the title *Alphabet de Mademoiselle Lili*.

Library of Congress Catalog Card No. 74-85219

Manufactured in the United States of America.

BOOK AND JACKET DESIGN BY BENTE HAMANN

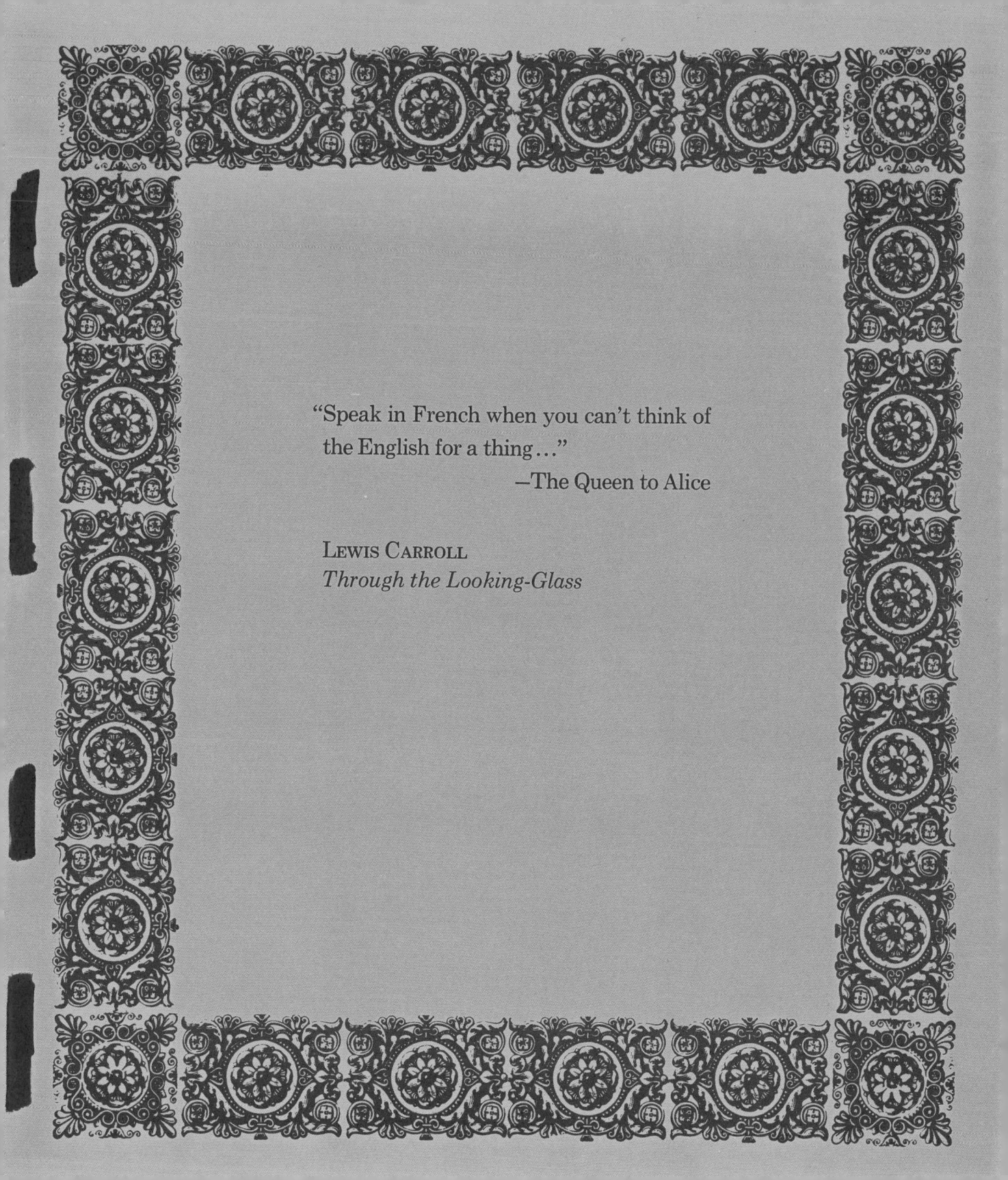

"Speak in French when you can't think of the English for a thing…"
—The Queen to Alice

LEWIS CARROLL
Through the Looking-Glass

*A*nne, Antoine et leur petit *agneau*
sont bons *amis*; l'*agneau* est
aussi gentil qu'eux.

Anne, Antoine and their little lamb
are good friends; the lamb is
as nice as they are.

amitié (f.)
friendship

ange (m.)
angel

abeille (f.)
bee

aile (f.)
wing

*B*rigitte, *en prenant son déjeuner,
n'oublie pas les petits oiseaux.*

While Brigitte eats her lunch, she
does not forget the little birds.

bonté (f.)
kindness

bec (m.)
beak

bouche (f.)
mouth

bras (m.)
arm

beurre (m.)
butter

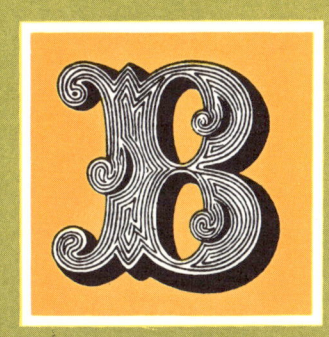

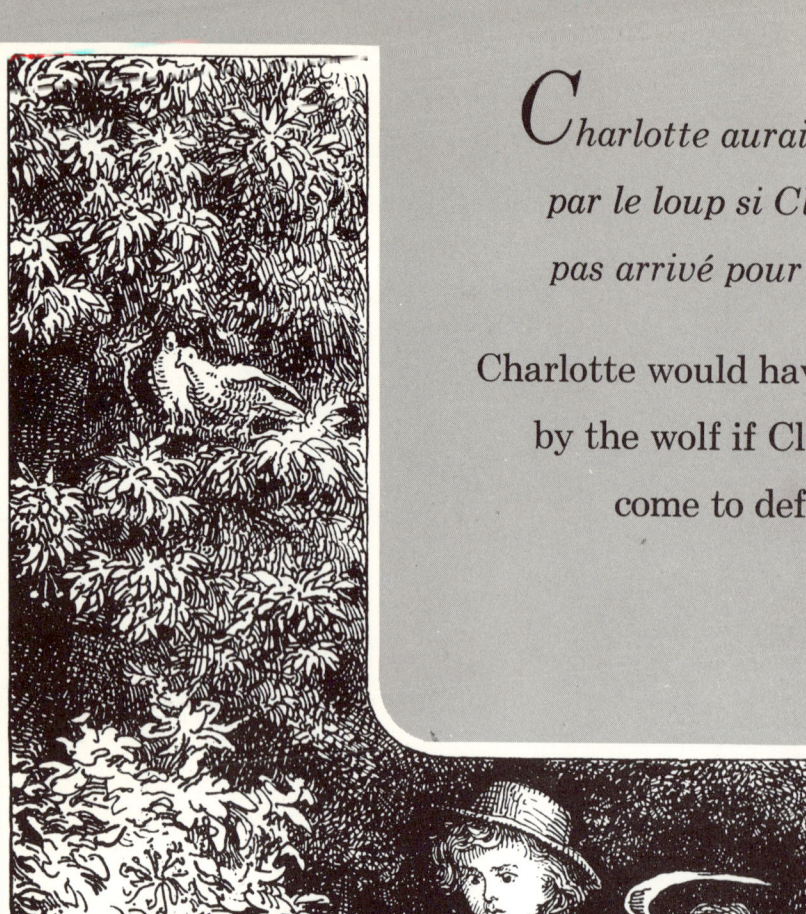

Charlotte aurait été attaquée par le loup si Claude n'était pas arrivé pour la défendre.

Charlotte would have been attacked by the wolf if Claude had not come to defend her.

colombe (f.)
dove

champignon (m.)
mushroom

cheveu (m.)
hair

chapeau (m.)
hat

courage (m.)
courage

Denis est un bon garçon; il fait
ses devoirs pour demain.
La leçon est un peu difficile.

Dennis is a good boy; he is doing
his homework for tomorrow.
The lesson is a little difficult.

dictionnaire (m.)
dictionary

daim (m.)
deer

dahlia (m.)
dahlia (flower)

dindon (m.)
turkey

doigt (m.)
finger

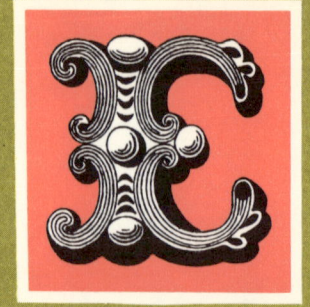

échelle (f.)
step-ladder

écureuil (m.)
squirrel

effroi (m.)
fright

épaule (f.)
shoulder

Emile est tombé en dénichant les petits oiseaux. Son frère va les remettre dans leur nid.

Emile fell while taking the little birds out of the nest. His brother is going to put them back in their nest.

François est le fils du fermier. Quand il est fatigué, il fait un somme dans le foin.

François is the farmer's son. When he is tired, he takes a nap in the hay.

faisan (m.)
pheasant

figue (f.)
fig

fraise (f.)
strawberry

feuille (f.)
leaf

fouine (f.)
marten

Georges se dépêche d'amener du grain pour nourrir son cheval, qui a faim.

George hurries to bring grain to feed his hungry horse.

guêpe (f.)
wasp

groseille (f.)
currant (berry)

gentiane (f.)
gentian (flower)

gamin (m.)
urchin

genou (m.)
knee

goût (m.)
taste

H

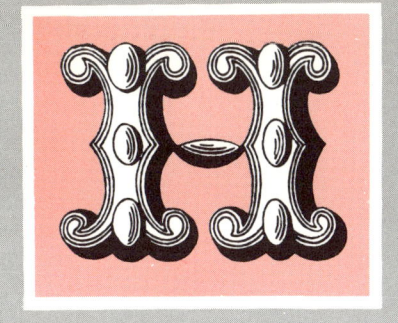

Henriette et sa grand-mère paraissent très surprises. Que pensez-vous qu'il soit arrivé?

Henrietta and her grandmother seem very surprised.

What do you think has happened?

hirondelle (f.)
swallow (bird)

hibou (m.)
owl

hareng (m.)
herring

héron (m.)
heron

herbe (f.)
grass

Isidore n'est pas assez grand pour sauter le fossé. Mais il trouve moyen de s'en tirer.

Isidore is not big enough to jump the ditch. But he finds a way to get across.

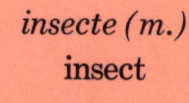

insecte (m.)
insect

iris (m.)
iris (flower)

ipomée (f.)
moonflower
(morning-glory)

île (f.)
island

*J*ean et Jacques sont des camarades. Ils sont aussi joyeux l'un que l'autre de se revoir.

Jean and Jacques are the very best of friends. They are both happy to see each other again.

joie (f.)
joy

jacquot (m.)
Polly (parrot)

jasmin (m.)
jasmine (flower)

jambe (f.)
leg

joujou (m.)
toy

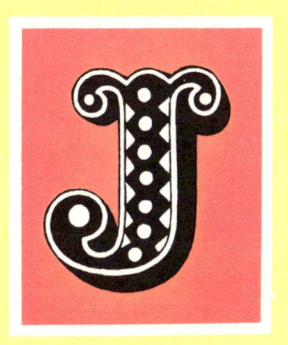

Kristine, Karen et Katharine sont sœurs.
Elles prient pour que leur mère
souffrante recouvre la santé.

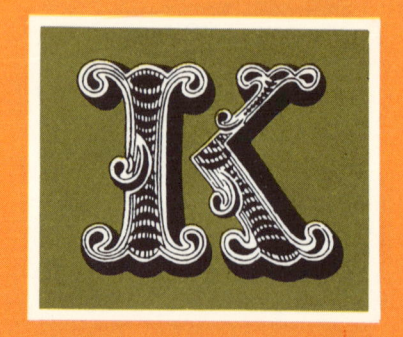

K

Kristine, Karen and Katharine are sisters.
They are praying
for their sick
mother
to become well.

kilomètre (m.)
kilometer

kangourou (m.)
kangaroo

kayak (m.)
Eskimo canoe

In French no first names start with "K", so non-French first names were used.   Words in glossary not pictured.

L

Louis revient vers sa mère et reçoit des louanges pour son travail.

Louis returns to his mother and gets praise for his work.

lune (f.)
moon

lapin (m.)
rabbit

lézard (m.)
lizard

lierre (m.)
ivy

lèvre (f.)
lip

M

*Martin est très vilain.
Il fait peur au
pauvre mouton.*

Martin
is very naughty.
He scares
the poor sheep.

montagne (f.)
mountain

moineau (m.)
sparrow

marronnier (m.)
chestnut-tree

maïs (m.)
corn

maison (f.)
house

Nicole, la nourrice, a délaissé la petite Nanette, qui est tombée et s'est fait mal.

Nicole, the nurse, did not look after little Nanette, who fell down and hurt herself.

nid (m.)
nest

navet (m.)
turnip

noix (f.)
nut

nuage (m.)
cloud

négligence (f.)
neglect

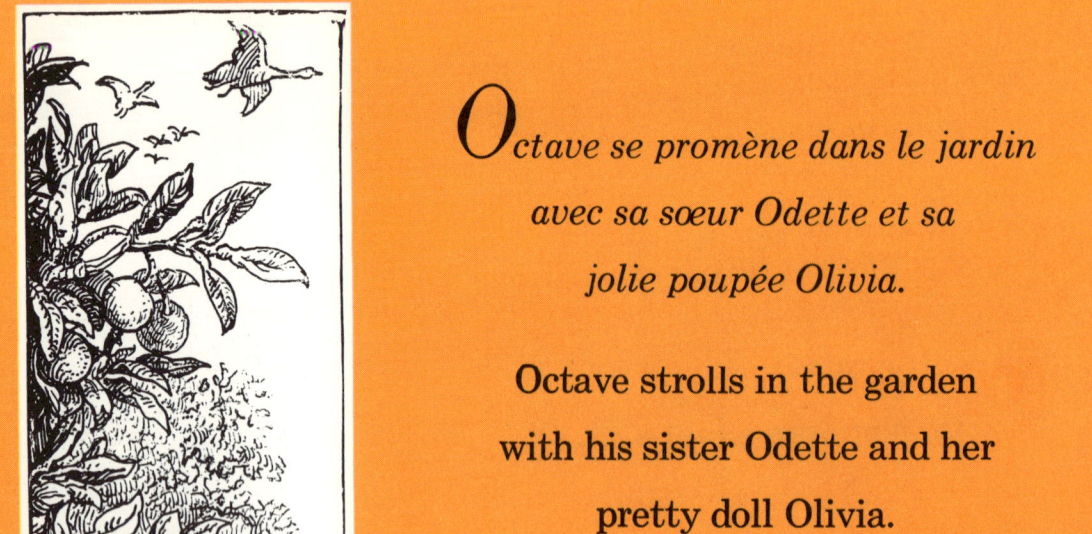

Octave se promène dans le jardin avec sa sœur Odette et sa jolie poupée Olivia.

Octave strolls in the garden with his sister Odette and her pretty doll Olivia.

oiseaux (m. pl.)
birds

orange (f.)
orange

ombrelle (f.)
parasol

œil (m.)
eye

oreille (f.)
ear

*P*auline, les chats et le petit oiseau aiment tous se laver.

Pauline, the cats and the little bird all love washing themselves.

propreté (f.)
cleanliness

prune (f.)
plum

papillon (m.)
butterfly

perroquet (m.)
parrot

pomme (f.)
apple

poire (f.)
pear

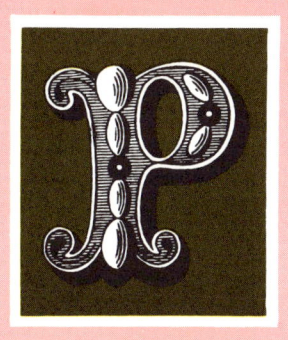

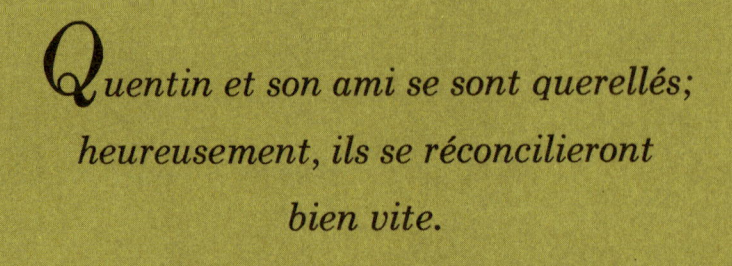

*Q*uentin et son ami se sont querellés;
heureusement, ils se réconcilieront
bien vite.

Quentin has quarreled with his friend;
but luckily they will make up
right away.

quenouille (f.)
spindle for spinning

quille (f.)
bowling pin

queue (f.)
tail, line

quoi?
what?

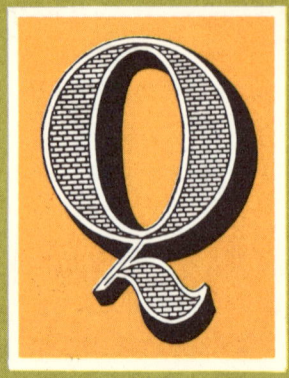

*R*obert et Richard regardent le renard,
qui voudrait manger les raisins,
mais ne peut pas les attraper.

Robert and Richard are looking at the fox,
who would like to eat the grapes,
but cannot reach them.

rire
to laugh

rat (m.)
rat

répondre
to answer

rue (f.)
street

Suzanne est au lit avec un rhume.
Sa mère lui donne une potion.

Susan is in bed with a cold.
Her mother gives her medicine.

sucre (m.)
sugar

singe (m.)
monkey

serpent (m.)
snake, serpent

souris (f.)
mouse

soir (m.)
evening

Thérèse embrasse sa mère
avant d'aller se coucher.

Theresa kisses her mother
before going to bed.

tendresse (f.)
tenderness

terre (f.)
earth

tulipe (f.)
tulip

tournesol (m.)
sunflower

trèfle (m.)
clover,
shamrock

Ursule fait le ménage, mais sa mère devra sans doute l'aider.

Ursula is doing the housework, but her mother will probably have to help her.

ustensile (m.)
tool, utensil

urne (f.)
urn

utile
useful

l'union fait la force
unity makes strong

Valentine se regarde dans le miroir.
Elle paraît très satisfaite.

Valentine looks at herself in the mirror.
She seems very pleased.

voile (m.)
veil

vigne (f.)
vine

vanité (f.)
vanity

verre (m.)
glass

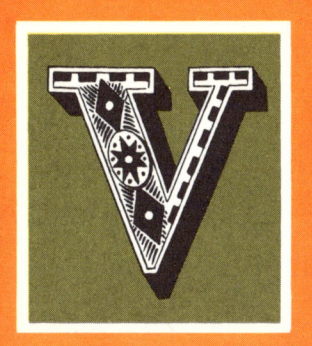

W

*Wilhelmine
ne sait pas
jouer au whist,
mais elle aime regarder
son père y jouer.*

Wilhelmina
does not know
how to play whist,
but she loves
to watch her
father playing.

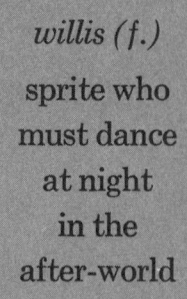

willis (f.)
sprite who
must dance
at night
in the
after-world

In French no first names start with "W", so a non-French first name was used.

*X*avier est un petit berger qui, nous l'espérons, donnera un morceau de bretzel à son chien.

Xavier is a little shepherd who, we hope, will give a piece of pretzel to his dog.

Xerxès*
King of Persia
(*c.* 519-465 B.C.)

xérès (m.)
sherry wine

xylographe (m.)*
wood engraver

* Not pictured.

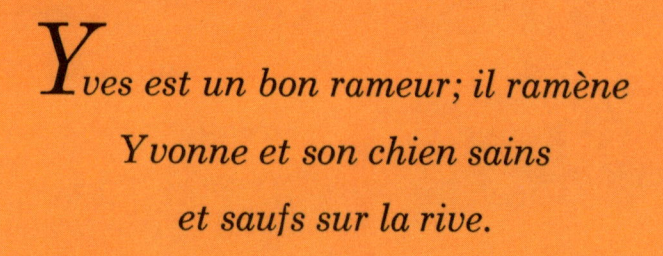

*Yves est un bon rameur; il ramène
Yvonne et son chien sains
et saufs sur la rive.*

Yves is a good rower; he returns
Yvonne and her dog to shore
safe and sound.

yeux (m. pl.)
eyes

yole (f.)
small rowboat

yacht (m.) *
yacht

*Not pictured.

Zélie est une très bonne couturière. Elle brode un mouchoir pour l'anniversaire de son grand-père.

Zelia is very good at sewing. She embroiders a handkerchief for her grandfather's birthday.

zèle (m.)
zeal

zéphyr (m.)
zephyr (west wind)

zibeline (f.)
sable

LES ABRÉVIATIONS
THE ABBREVIATIONS

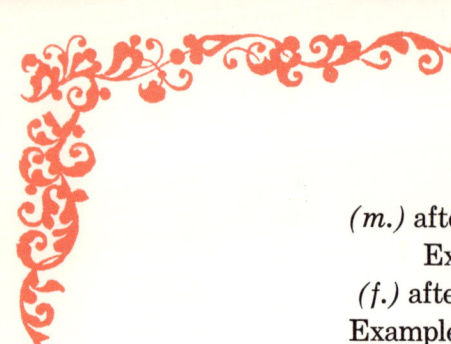

(m.) after a noun indicates the masculine gender: *le, un*.
Example: *le chat* (the cat), *un chat* (a cat).
(f.) after a noun indicates the feminine gender: *la, une*.
Example: *la maison* (the house), *une maison* (a house).
(pl.) after a noun indicates plural.
(sing.) after a noun indicates singular.

LES NOMBRES
THE NUMBERS

1. un   2. deux   3. trois   4. quatre   5. cinq
6. six   7. sept   8. huit   9. neuf   10. dix

LES JOURS THE DAYS	LES MOIS THE MONTHS	LES MOIS THE MONTHS
dimanche (m.) Sunday	*janvier (m.)* January	*juillet (m.)* July
lundi (m.) Monday	*février (m.)* February	*août (m.)* August
mardi (m.) Tuesday	*mars (m.)* March	*septembre (m.)* September
mercredi (m.) Wednesday	*avril (m.)* April	*octobre (m.)* October
jeudi (m.) Thursday		
vendredi (m.) Friday	*mai (m.)* May	*novembre (m.)* November
samedi (m.) Saturday	*juin (m.)* June	*décembre (m.)* December

LA TABLE

1. La nappe
2. La soupière
3. Le couvercle
4. La louche
5. L'huilier (m.)
6. La salière
7. Le rond de serviette
8. Le verre à vin
9. La bouteille
10. Le bouchon
11. La cuillère
12. L'assiette (f.)
13. La serviette
14. La fourchette
15. Le couteau
16. Le casse-noisette
17. Le tire-bouchon
18. Le dessous de plat
19. La corbeille à pain
20. La sonnette
21. La chaise

Drawing from *circa* 1880, artist unknown.

a b c d e f
g h i j k l
m n o p q r
s t u v w x
y z 1 2 3 4
5 6 7 8 9 0